To Mirte and Seppe,
who make me rediscover the world every single day.
— Jan Leyssens

Originally published as *De ontdekking van de dinosaurussen*
in Belgium and the Netherlands by Clavis Uitgeverij, 2020
English translation from the Dutch by Clavis Publishing Inc., New York

Visit us on the Web at www.clavis-publishing.com.

The Discovery of the Dinosaurs written by Jan Leyssens and illustrated by Joachim Sneyers

ISBN 978-1-60537-719-3

This book was printed in May 2021 at Nikara, M. R. Štefánika 858/25, 963 01 Krupina, Slovakia.

First Edition
10 9 8 7 6 5 4 3 2 1

The Discovery
of the
Dinosaurs

Written by Jan Leyssens
Illustrated by Joachim Sneyers

Clavis
NEW YORK

It isn't entirely clear when the first dinosaur fossils and bones were dug up. However, more than two thousand years ago, Chinese scholars wrote about the so-called dragon bones they had found. They haven't been preserved, but many scientists think that those bones may have belonged to dinosaurs.

In 1676, Robert Plot, an English archaeological museum curator, stumbled upon an enormous femur. Because he didn't know of any animal that could grow so big, he first thought it was from an old species of elephant or a giant. One hundred and fifty years later, they discovered the bone probably once belonged to a Megalosaurus dinosaur.

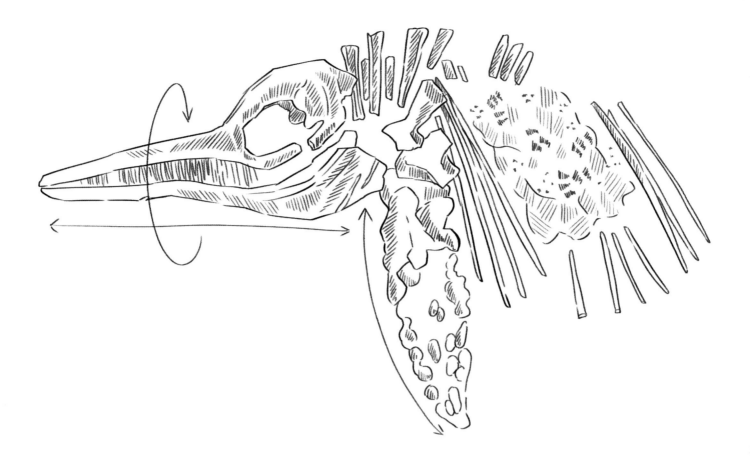

At the beginning of the nineteenth century, Mary Anning wanted to earn extra money for her family. Together with her brother and mother, she looked along the English coast for fossils to sell. When she was twelve, Mary found her first dinosaur skeleton: the first complete Ichthyosaurus ever found. Between 1811 and 1830, Mary would find several more dinosaur skeletons.

Mary's fossils captured everyone's imagination. Until that moment, the idea that giant lizard-like creatures once inhabited our lands and seas was unthinkable. During this time, Mary was not admitted to a university because she was a woman. However, her discovery made her one of the most important fossil hunters ever.

To make the newly discovered animals more tangible to the people of London, paleontologist Richard Owen wanted to make life-sized images of them. That's why he brought various fossils, including the ones Mary had found, to artist Benjamin Waterhouse Hawkins' studio.

Under the watchful eye of Richard, who had the most recent knowledge of dinosaurs, Benjamin was able to design and build the sculptures. The work took three years.

On 31 December 1853, Benjamin invited the most important paleontologists and scientists to a New Year's dinner. They dined in the sculpture of a dinosaur called an Iguanodon.

In the months that followed, he put thirty-three dinosaur statues in London's Crystal Palace Park, where they're still on display today.

It was also Richard Owen who invented the word "dinosaur" in 1842. It means "terrible lizard" in Greek, and that's also exactly how dinosaurs were portrayed. Dinosaurs were depicted as slow, ponderous animals crawling through the mud on their bellies, and resembled crocodiles.

In 1967, American university student Robert Bakker and his professor dug up a new kind of dinosaur called a Velociraptor. They noticed that some dinosaur skeletons looked more like sporty birds than ponderous lizards.

Coincidentally, Robert was not only a promising paleontologist, but also a good artist. His drawings didn't depict the Velociraptor as a crawling lizard, but as the sprinting dinosaur we know today.

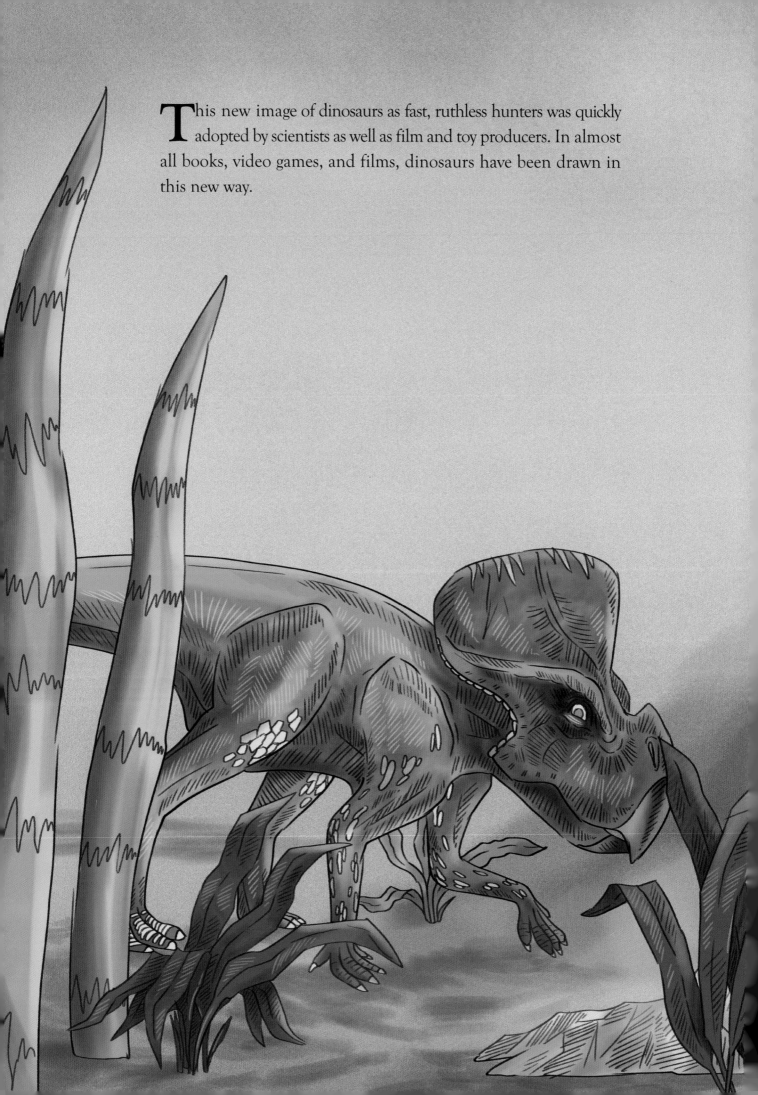

This new image of dinosaurs as fast, ruthless hunters was quickly adopted by scientists as well as film and toy producers. In almost all books, video games, and films, dinosaurs have been drawn in this new way.

26 m

Polacanthus

5 m

Tyrannosaurus

As more fossils were discovered and more research was performed, there was a growing certainty that many different types of dinosaurs had existed in the past. Both slow and fast dinosaurs, lizard-like dinosaurs, feathered dinosaurs, giant Diplodocuses, and Velociraptors that weren't much bigger than a chicken were found.

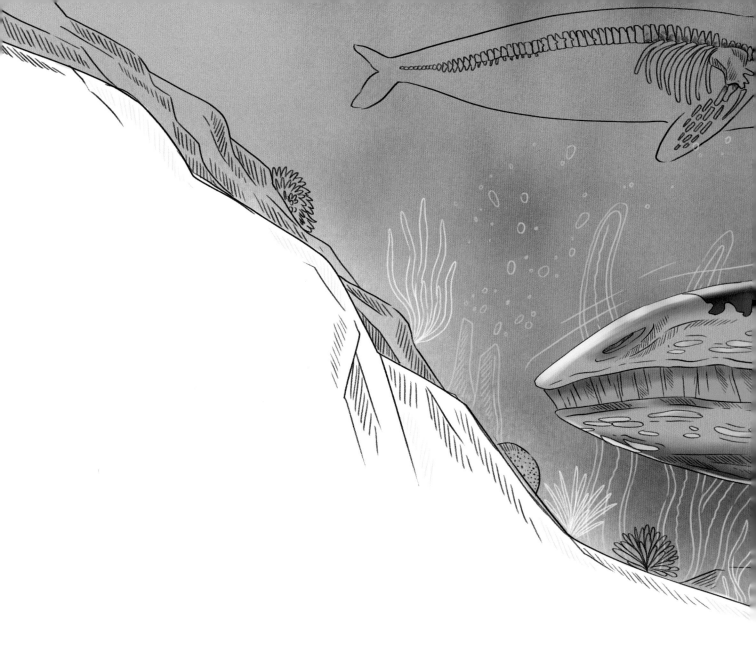

The hardest thing about drawing something you've never seen is that you can only base your drawing on whatever is available. In this case, the drawings were only based on skeletons. However, dinosaur skeletons were often puzzled together incorrectly, resulting in wrong images. Indeed, we can roughly guess where the muscles must have been, but how can we be sure about the size and weight?

Think of a whale. Its body is mostly fat. Whoever uses the skeleton of a whale as a model for a drawing, without ever having seen a whale, would probably draw a very strange fish with a thick head and a long, thin tail.

Nowadays, more and more paleontologists try to depict dinosaurs in different forms. They may be depicted with or without fat, in different colors, with feathers, or as a lizard. We'll probably never know what dinosaurs really looked like.

Because of the skeletons Mary found, and the countless artists who brought the dinosaurs back to life in their drawings and sculptures, we can still form an image of the gigantic creatures that walked through our forests two hundred million years ago.